The Ebbing Tide

Neil Huxter

The Ebbing Tide

A Collection of Sonnets

The Boars Hill Press

First published in Great Britain 2002
by The Boars Hill Press, Heron Wood,
Jarn Way, Boars Hill, Oxford OX1 5JF

© Neil Huxter 2002

All rights reserved. No part of this publication
may be reproduced, stored in a retrieval system,
or transmitted, in any form or by any means,
electronic, mechanical, photocopying, recording
or otherwise, without the prior permission
in writing of the publishers.

A CIP catalogue record for this book is available
from the British Library

ISBN 0 9543306 0 9

Designed and typeset by The Stonesfield Press,
Peakes House, Stonesfield, Witney, Oxon

Printed and bound in Great Britain
by Information Press, Eynsham, Oxford

*For Angela
with love*

CONTENTS

Preface *ix*
The Ebbing Tide *1–18*
Sonnets from Littondale *19–34*
Snow on Quinag *35–44*
Big Grant the Bard *45–51*
Türkiye *52–55*
When you are Old *56–59*
By Semer Water *60–77*
The Jackdaw Flock *78–84*
Karayel was Blowing *85–92*
The Falling Rain *93–103*
Autumn Bush Clover *104–113*
The Three-Day-Old Moon *114–116*

PREFACE

When Slender in *The Merry Wives of Windsor* says 'I had rather than forty shillings I had my Book of Songs and Sonnets here,' he wants help in courting Mistress Anne Page. My collection of sonnets meets my desire to see some of my poems in print and reminds me of the cost and trepidation that have gone into making them.

The reader will notice that these poems have as their subjects Norfolk, Littondale, Gairloch, Sutherland and places abroad such as Troy, Istanbul and Antalya. Some were written in these different places, but most here on Boars Hill in the relative peace of my study. That they are all sonnets may be explained in this way: at busy times it suited me to use a form to which I had become accustomed over the years. In the modern age, it seemed permissible to bring in topics and instances of every sort and to be both formal and informal in the same poem.

The use of the expression *Niru sama*, 'Mr Neil', indicates supposed interjections by the renowned and supremely beautiful ninth-century poetess Ono no Komachi. The name Komachi is now generally used to indicate a beautiful woman in Japan. There are references to Japanese poetry scattered through the book; for example, the last two lines of the sonnet on p. 65 refer to a poem sent to a lady by Ariwara no Narihira,

PREFACE

the great ninth-century poet and lover, and her reply (see *Tales from Ise*, section 123).

There are ten sonnets at the end of this volume taken from the 1111 *tanka* of the *Kokinshû*, and three that use poems from Book 7 of the *Manyôshû*. In these sonnets, I generally used an introductory quartet, then my version of two Japanese poems in two quartets and then a closing couplet for a coda.

I should like to thank Simon Haviland of the Stonesfield Press for expert editorial points and queries. I fear many more changes have had to be made than he originally anticipated when he saw typed pages of work I had done this year.

Neil Huxter
Boars Hill, Wednesday 31 July 2002

THE EBBING TIDE

Monday 23 July 2001

Folk on this coast go out with the ebbing tide,
Leave like old boats faint outlines in the mud:
Salty samphire stems refresh their fading blood,
Pickling through winter keeps their feelings blithe!
Green July's long days bring hours of mowing,
February warm fires when southeasters blow,
Font carved; churched oars and lobster pots
Represent the tarry fisherman's lot.
Black-headed gulls bicker along brown creeks,
Shrill oystercatchers background the saltings' music,
While scythe-winged swifts snatch their insect pick,
As curing sheds disperse their kipper reek.
Halyards clatter above the salt marsh maze
Beyond the whelk sheds at Brancaster Staithe.

THE EBBING TIDE

Friday 27 July 2001

The stone slates are sized down, the smaller
To the top, the bigger towards the eaves,
Fish scales, bird feathers: half-anxious unease
Delighting in meadow, wood and river.
William Morys sumtyme fermer of Cokyswell,
And *Jehane the wyf of William Morys:*
A glance like water brimming with the sky,
Her genius was beauty's sovereign spell.
From Alvescot and Stanton Harcourt she stemmed,
Delightfully at home at Kenelm's Cot:
Pale Helen of Troy's loveliness her lot,
Long, glorious hair chunk-cut to be tamed.
We're shielded by women and heroes untold
From winds that sweep the winter-bitten wold.

THE EBBING TIDE

Monday 6 August 2001

Rain falls on grey Kelmscott by the green Thames;
Concrete souvenirs of nineteen-forty,
Two solid pill-boxes do their duty
Untested on the north bank, still the same.
On our wet terrace dahlias stand tall,
Begonias spill orange-red cascades:
A pair of living jewels now display
Dress most suitable for resplendent balls.
Pavones cristati Bert and Rosie,
Two common peafowl, have adopted us,
Spend the night in an oak-tree without fuss,
Peer through French windows, alert and nosy.
They take bread from my hand, sun on the roof,
Terrace and gravel, beautiful and aloof.

THE EBBING TIDE

Wednesday 8 August 2001

Rain, sun and wind in burning August,
The bees buzz hungry to fill up their store,
Other insects build up the peafowls' score,
Who place in foraging their rewarded trust.
Queenly Rosalind summoned Bertram
To the roof with her lonely aw-h aw-h call;
He responded slowly, part-enthralled,
Flew up and stalked the tiles like the Great Cham.
For William Morris Iceland turned out tops:
To the Geysers he could no longer go,
Beautiful blue boiling holes, uncanny so;
In Laxdale his usual high spirits dropped.
Rest from the wind and sunset cheered him up,
Where Olaf Peacock saw to ewes and tups.

THE EBBING TIDE

Friday 17 August 2001

A<small>LL</small> background sounds made beautiful and clear,
Combine Harvesters roaring in the fields,
The Deepdale yeoman binds his corn-sheaf yield,
Rosalind calls the mate she holds so dear.
Olaf the Peacock or Kjartan Olafsson,
The best-looking man ever born in Iceland;
Helga the Fair, the loveliest that swanned,
Golden hair her body's caparison;
Hallgerd Longlegs, who brought three husbands down,
Thief-eyed! I'm happy with what I've got,
Not a little, certainly not a lot,
Wielding a pencil, private scribbler grown,
For reward, all the beauty that's been known,
Poised in loveliness, living statements shown!

THE EBBING TIDE

Friday 17 August 2001

'THE skald is not quite used to riding then!',
   The Lithend bonder said, when Morris mounted,
More Icelandico; his body measured
His length on the turf, wrong-sided again.
The turf at the Geysers was littered
With feathers, birds' wings, mutton-bones, paper;
He found deep holes of beautiful blue water,
Where they boiled fish, uncannily weighted.
He felt very low in salmoned Laxdale,
Alone he knew how sad cold Iceland felt;
Rest from the wind and coloured sunset spelt
Relief, red and green, rain clouds down the dale.
Olaf and Thorgerd loved each other,
Herd's Holt housed his cows, ewes and wethers.

THE EBBING TIDE

Thursday 23 August 2001

The peafowl preen themselves on the terrace,
Together after a long day apart;
Loud barking, sudden noises make them start;
Moulting done, he'll swell his stately carriage.
We're given golden olive oil, herb-enriched,
From blue sea'd Greece, and olive oil soap;
Odysseus, after two salt days and nights, soaped
With the oil a Princess sent to smooth his skin.
The Coxes brought gifts from Cephalonia,
Fragrant ouzo, clouding the cold water,
Tasted with black olives! Zeus's daughters,
And Memory's, let your strengths win here.
Ionian Robola, lemon white,
Accompany Poseidon's fish tonight.

THE EBBING TIDE

Friday 14 & Monday 17 September 2001

WINTER'S witches hold covens to hex bright summer,
    Hecla's hordes broom-stick down the chilly north-
    west wind;
Before them fly the brent geese, vigorous flock aligned,
And falls of fleeing snipe, northern springtime drummers.
The kettle whistles like chilly winds in the eaves,
The cool radiators come on, pump-infused with warmth:
Well-insulated seals arch in the sun's strength,
A brettle of seagulls harvest where herring fry seethe.
Beside green-patched grass where a bothy once stood,
A solitary jack snipe goes up from the marsh;
This lonely hillside expanse wet walkers find harsh,
Attuned creatures sense the solitude all good.
Striped camouflage blends the migrant snipe with his scene,
Human hearts weight such moments with all that's been.

THE EBBING TIDE

Wednesday 19 September 2001

In this empty place the wind holds sway,
A haunt of lurking trolls, who hide themselves away;
Clinging mist clouds cover Cuinneag, there's no way
Red deer are to be seen, securely veiled they graze.
Massed deer take over the Bealach road at night
Between Loch Assynt's long reaches and bypassed Kylesku;
Horned stags, sleek hinds, unfocused yearlings endue
Bright headlights with live substance, by-ordinar sight.
Red grouse, white-winged *tàrmachan* secrete themselves
On grey-stoned hillsides among sweet blueberries;
White bog asphodel ghosts show how seasons vary,
The hill's quietness, sunlit, tells of lives shelved.
A pair of herons follow their unchanging law,
Foraging fresh sustenance on a rocky shore.

THE EBBING TIDE

Monday 8 October 2001

We're long weeks past Stookie Sunday when the cut corn stands,
We live in a green land, circling seasons attuned:
They say, 'There's aye some water whaur the stirkie drouns!'
Now we must heap pain on a parched, hungry land.
A weighted tractor tracks stripes on the brown plough,
Threatening winds blow, stripping past summer's green trees:
Boreas spares fleeced sheep but old men find no ease,
A girl anoints her soft skin with olive oil now.
Youthful Jane, in a steaming bath, now shows
Her naked perfection, heat-controlled.
Never slight folk whom painful poverty keeps cold,
Feed sufferers who have no fruitful place to go.
When leaves on a fig's top shoot match a crow's footprint,
Then try the sea, but in hot summer sail without stint.

THE EBBING TIDE

Tuesday 23 October 2001

Virid shoot-blades of winter wheat green the brown plough,
Like the grass seeds I've planted in this bare-patched wood;
Coated buds wait on the willows, patient spring's goods,
As we slide into winter past effort endowed.
The Eel of the Heather still seeks his scented nest,
But sub-Arctic storms warn him to choose a warm earth-bed;
White seagulls drift in loose formation overhead,
Their side-slipping glides seeming to require no rest.
You're more beautiful than the common sons of men,
Appearing a crowded city's bright ornament;
All that loveliness sets you high above dissent,
Raising the standard higher and higher again.
Please be my flaybogle, keep swarming spooks away,
Winter boggarts and trolls, may they fear night and day!

THE EBBING TIDE

Wednesday 24 October 2001

This abundant season proves *pomosus*, full of fruit,
We give Pomona thanks and Artemis, goddess
Of the chase, for partridge, pheasant, snipe dressed
For our autumn tables, gratification suits.
The mass of Arncliffe Clouder draws down the rain clouds,
Half doubling the fall of inches to bridged Burnsall;
Under Kilnsey's rock overhangs wet climbers sprawl
On ropes, using the skills modern techniques allow.
'But grose and gredie wittes which grope but on the
    ground'
May not rise so high, their physical chemistry
Holds them earthbound, each in their living mystery,
Keen to discover what correlations abound.
Fortunate those who taste a love match of their kind,
'For they do holde continually a heaven in their minde.'

THE EBBING TIDE

Friday 26 October 2001

O UR Neapolitan cyclamen are growing
Colourfully in pots safe from Boars Hill's wild pigs,
Who'd snuffle out their tuberous rootstocks, where twigs
Mark the trees moving to the autumn's wind soughing.
Did the studious philosopher save himself
Walking on the hill, from the snorting wild boar's charge,
By thrusting his Aristotle, reason writ large,
Into those jaws? Power is the Stagirite's pledge.
Who wrote: 'With petrarke to compare there may no
  wight'?
He wrote: 'But yet I wote full well where is a file
To frame a learned man:' her presence brings a smile,
Seeing 'eche line of just proportion to her height'.
If hypercritical Momus downe discended,
He'd not once say: 'Lo this may be amended!'

THE EBBING TIDE

Tuesday 30 October 2001

These warm October days are bright with burnished
  gold:
Poets 'attaine to knowe the misteries devine
Of perfite love wherto hie wittes of knowledge do incline',
Those subtleties of loving that are felt not told.
Lovely thaumaturge, what magic you work on me!
'For when that in my heart I fele that dyd me greve
With one imbracing of her armes she might me sone releve'
Graced with the fullness of your soft plenity!
Touching 'her corall lippes would straightaways make me
  gladde',
Soft yew berries that string up England's springing bow!
Your enchantment's spells no circumlocution know,
Promising shared delights beneath my hunting plaid!
As the mass of Arncliffe Clouder draws down the rain
  clouds,
To your magnetic north compass needles are vowed!

THE EBBING TIDE

Friday 9 November 2001

Raising their gabble-ratchet the wild geese raced
The winter storm, cold winds bringing dark banks of cloud,
Freezing rain, stinging hail, round balls of sleet, snow shrouds!
Let your chin sink into the tartan scarf's embrace.
On the Ridgeway chacking fieldfares forage hedgerows;
Unfazed by us they love lonely places,
Search the green pasture of Segsbury Camp, no stasis,
Busy and noisy, every way at once they go.
No busy bees visit sky-blue borage these days,
Storing no bee-bread in their sheltered cells;
The peacock's growing green feathers, where the rain fell,
Show bronzed brown, those serried blue eyes will amaze.
Every way at once the lolloping shot-struck hare sprawls
As my heart does, stiff-nippled Artemis' thrall!

Wednesday 21 November 2001

The peafowl lie in the leaves on the drive,
Snug on the gravel, camouflaged gems;
His blue neck forecasts summer, dragonflies named
Adder's-bolts, and weeks when adder's-grasses thrive.
Ten syllable lines come naturally
To English ears, Marlowe, William Shakespeare:
Hesper, guide me home when dark skies weigh near,
To warmth and shelter and the rich day's tally.
Frequent coveys of grey partridge scurry
Over stubble and brown plough, tangled fields
Feeding them seeds. May the season's ample yield
Keep them flying in a curved wing flurry.
At dusk mallard squatter up, seeking skies
Filled with evening; home-fires call 'Come by!'

THE EBBING TIDE

Friday 4 January 2002

Bring me cold *sake* to spice the New Year:
Out on the stiff grass white snow lies frozen,
A crow bathes alone where the ice is broken.
Will First Day offerings bring us to *Pernglair*?
Devil's Apron, *noshi*, and roast *nori*,
Arame and *wakame*, a seaweed spree:
Cold kelp moves tally, swayed by the salt sea,
Warmed up at home tells another story.
Father Christmas brought me blood pressure pills,
Reducing the outflow to extremities;
Urine specimens and an ECG,
Procedures to define the body's ills.
The peafowl are besieged by hungry birds,
Maintaining this mixed corn is rightly theirs!

THE EBBING TIDE

Tuesday 16 April 2002

By the iron gate dog-laurel flambeaux
Release clustered scent in their treed shelter;
At the open field's edge the sun turns melter
Of frozen white dew, where the cold most shows.
Hugh Grosvenor, Life Guards, in 'forty-seven
Was killed in an armoured car accident
On the Ridgeway, aged nineteen: where his years went
The loud A34 adds a noise level leaven.
Below Quiet Settlement Hill rooks still caw
In the grove where the Roman Temple stood
Near the silent burial grounds; the spirit's goods
Assert light for shadows the long years draw.
Dust rises swirling from the trodden track,
Numen inest, there is no final lack.

SONNETS FROM LITTONDALE

Friday 27 August 1993

CAN bad bogies find it? Kingsley's Vendale.
Grouse chir-burst, curve-winging over heather:
Safe from the worst onslaughts of bad weather,
Through green pastures Skirfare tracks a peaty trail.
From Malham Tarn House over the grey moor
Charles walked to Bridge End, where dippers nest,
Brown trout guard pools, grey wagtails never rest;
In fine weather they took tea out of doors.
To another cottage, hidden away
In the deep fork of Amerdale, followed
The White Doe, stepping Darnbrook's pathless way.
Up past the grouse butts by Pen-y-Ghent House
We climbed, back through heathery hollows,
Splashed into the beck pool for a cool douse.

SONNETS FROM LITTONDALE

Saturday 28 August 1993

PEREGRINES scour Blue Scar behind the inn,
Above the shippon where small Meg was born;
By one stone wall our sheepdog Bess launched
Into Cowside Beck, ladder-stiles up to the chin.
Scented smoke drifting, curlews call, pure peace:
Oystercatchers fluting overhead pare
The quietness; by the curve of brown Skirfare
Sand martins nest in their annual reach.
'Ah! Who could think that sadness here hath sway?'
Sharp pain, cold fear? The stone slab roofs slope close,
Protecting the long green of an older day.
Here Middle Lane's grey stone walls stand preserved:
A list in St Oswalds's towered church shows
The arms and men that at Flodden Field served.

SONNETS FROM LITTONDALE

Monday 6 September 1993

ENGLAND'S September: under cool green leaves
Night's badgers have nuzzled coated chestnuts;
Feathery rosebay hides rabbit scuts,
Crab apples lie under the laden tree.
Meg sniffs the scented air, full hunter's moon:
Admiral, are you sleeping there below
Off Coronel? Against the sunset glow
Kennelled Rock accompanied him home.
Beef, mustard, Yorkshire ale: Kingsley climbed out
Of Magdalene to go fishing; Brooke dined
In hall with A. C. Benson, perhaps on trout.
For centuries falcons have nested in the scar
Over the brown beck; seasons aligned,
Past, present, future enfold us where we are.

SONNETS FROM LITTONDALE

Thursday 30 September 1993

WHERE I mowed yesterday fresh leaves lie strewn,
Across the wooden fence grey bonfire smoke trails,
Tracks in the heavy dew our wet boots entail:
Blue sky, white cloud, summer's semblance at noon.
Beaumont and Fletcher tell how the gold sun
Comes to kiss the fruit in wealthy autumn;
Enriched in Keats, the season's bosom friend,
Mature, weights vines that round the thatch eaves run.
Black brush, the woman's hand you showed me, Komachi,
Indelible curves guiding the famed page,
Precise editing by Tsurayuki.
Now the ploughed field curves on the hillside,
Trees hold brocade, moonlights the sight engage,
From gold apples a grey squirrel scurries.

SONNETS FROM LITTONDALE

Tuesday 12 October 1993

KEITH DOUGLAS visited Boars Hill in the war
To see the Appletons in Masefield House,
Hill Crest. He said he was looking for a spouse,
Thinking of the pension, his death not far.
Raking up leaves this sunny afternoon,
Forking up sandstones by raspberry canes,
The bright sunlight turned to sudden rain,
After loud thunder, this season's tune.
Bo, that's darkening, *hi ga kureru*,
Day and year's darkening. Agrippa tells you
Wood fires assist, giving good spirits their cue.
Cornelius showed Surrey, Geraldine,
Couched reading his verse; Surrey gave Virgil his due,
Live translator; head short, the Seymours thought fine.

SONNETS FROM LITTONDALE

Thursday 11 August 1994

By Gozzard's Ford the gold wheat's harvested,
Where herded geese paddled the shallow stream.
Here Meg puts up pheasant, a spaniel's dream,
Rough shooting she'd find a sound investment.
Born in a shippon behind Arncliffe's inn,
She shows the hunter's look, those burning eyes;
Her nose examines leaves by the path's side,
She longs for search and springing to begin.
When Rock swam the creek, retrieving partridge,
He made no move, till Cradock showed which way;
Return trips through freezing water remade,
Eager to bring back dead trophies smartly.
Swallows chatter and swerve over the green,
By brown Skirfare's run a grey wagtail preens.

SONNETS FROM LITTONDALE

Monday 29 August 1994

THE screaming swift flock has stiff-winged south,
Robins crackle below red-tinged elders;
Aligned on telephone wires, swallows stir;
Muscular trout swirl, showing hungry mouths.
Meg swam in the Wharfe after plump mallard;
For a Bank Holiday, not many cars,
Mostly the brown river sweeps unscarred:
Hogback tombs in Burnsall are held by bears.
Below Kilnsey Crag the white marquees crowd,
Four-by-fours abound, the rain pashes down,
Straw bales form fences for preparing riders.
Long-maned shire horses, immaculate cows,
Gold Highland cattle pace slow-timed rounds:
A high place to herds Theocritos allowed.

SONNETS FROM LITTONDALE

Thursday 1 September 1994

FOUR goosanders in line trawl the Skirfare,
Their family group heads upstream fishing,
Brown-necked these days, saw-billed attrition;
First League, they are professional players.
At two hundred and sixty-two metres,
Race-horses gallop on Middleham Low Moor;
When windy winter comes, leaving High Moor,
Warm-jacketed jockeys perch high featly.
Marching to Virosidium, Rome's legions
Felt the cold wind blowing on Wether Fell,
Recalled the taste of wine from warmer regions.
Where white mushrooms stud the virid pasture,
Corralled rams wait for November's revels,
Deft swallows speed the peregrine's departure.

SONNETS FROM LITTONDALE

Friday 2 September 1994

THE evening star shines over Darnbrook Fell,
Wild duck scud to pastures beside Skirfare,
The tawny owl hoots softly by the scars;
Shining limestone reflects Bess' coat so well.
Studdleber Barn stands over Cowside Beck,
Where Bess swam, avoiding the high stone wall:
One goldfinch perches where the white stones sprawl,
A dipper low-flies Mill Holme without check.
Two heather grouse, killed six days ago,
Adorn the inn's kitchen, feathers plucked
Fall to the floor, hung aroma just so.
Kilnsey waters stretch from Netherside:
Sixty-five fishermen essay their luck
With seasonable flies, no casting wide.

SONNETS FROM LITTONDALE

Monday 4 September 1995

ON the high sheepwalk below Plover Hill,
Wide-viewed to Littondale, I recall Bess
Herding us. Four weeks dead now, her white bones rest
In her Boars Hill wood, bearing our love still.
Now Pat and Meg, Cap and Jed fetch the flock,
Light-boned and agile, high stone walls no hass,
Along tarred roads a casual last
Behind the slow Friesians' reachable hocks.
Small trout glide like shadows by the rock-pool side,
A grey heron flaps up by Cosh Beck ford,
In the tractor cab a spaniel rides.
Over Darnbrook Fell the evening star's bright,
Limestone walls still glow in Hesper's accord,
While memories live in love's magic night.

SONNETS FROM LITTONDALE

Saturday 9 September 1995

Hattie, aged two, asked if the rain wet Bess,
Now acorns and drops fall from cooler skies;
Bess loved sitting outside, while her nose tried
The air from the Downs, the downpour's glad guest.
She plunged into Cowside Beck, avoiding
Another stone wall, she was very pleased;
Snatched by Skirfare's swift current, only the lead
Saved her one April, below Ingle Dean.
In sunlight, my tractor roars overhead,
Now the greening grass has grown tall at last;
The compost heap gathers pelargonia heads.
You knew four generations, one dead,
In each day's loving trust you hold us fast,
While holly berries begin turning red.

SONNETS FROM LITTONDALE

Thursday 14 October 1993

'SEEING autumn flowers fade, my heart too
Withers away, though sadness' colour
Doesn't show; nobody sees my dolour.'
An editor wrote that, hard to do.
When the water level's high, you can't see
The bedrock sand of Shedding Tear River:
Unless the bank-side's dry, you'll never
Know what lies at the bottom: *okibi*.
'And by the fire help wast a sullen day,'
'Now that the Fields are dank, and ways are mire:'
Milton wrote that his own special way.
Gold and red of the leaves, under wet boots,
In bright sunlight; bring all that the heart desires,
Good food, wine, warmth, loving, poems that suit.

SONNETS FROM LITTONDALE

Tuesday 19 October 1993

If it were the soft sighs bush warblers sang
That stopped the petals falling, I myself
Would be highly pleased if only it helped
To utter notes just like that fine bird's song!
A lady-in-waiting wrote that poem.
Little cuckoos sing with the irises
In the month of May; I can merely guess
Love's patterns, so difficult to know 'em.
Flanky heifers have left the freezing pasture,
A sharp smell of staling, dark pats frozen hard;
No mad cow disease, what a disaster.
We walked White Horse Hill to the green camp,
High up the curved Downs; crows mobbed a buzzard
Over pastel fields, century-stamped.

SONNETS FROM LITTONDALE

Tuesday 20 April 1993

THE cock pheasant Meg put up among the graves
Round St Oswald's Church, crossed over the wall
To the water side. Ki saw pine trees stand tall,
And blossoming plum before River Bank Hall:
By the Yodo's shoals and pools he recalled
Who Prince Koretaka kept in his enclave:
If cherry trees had never put out blossom
In this world of ours, untroubling emotions
Would keep place in spring; no petalled commotion
On the scented breeze, just playing possum.
If only affection's thread stretched out
Along parting's path, the heart would not feel
So sad! Brown trout revolve the creaking reel,
Where thymy grayling sail, dorsal fin out.

SONNETS FROM LITTONDALE

Wednesday 21 April 1993

THOUGH the night is cold, I shall brush away
The first frost from the slope, where rime's settled;
Then on this grass pillow, placed on my mettle,
First of many, I'll sleep this night away.
If it hadn't been for the waterfall
Gushing through the rocks, I'd have reached my hand
To pick a branch of cherry blossom, grand
Sight for those who don't see it by the fall!
The brown river skirrs below wooded scars,
Rain on the fells makes the rapids foam white,
At the bridge foot dippers bob, awaiting parr.
None of the nine Hammond siblings married
Niru sama, dew vanishes when the sun's bright,
Down life's flowing river our names are carried.

SONNETS FROM LITTONDALE

Wednesday 19 April 1995

CHRIST'S arms and legs were nailed to the cross:
Leaves bust from the trees, scented petals shine bright,
The warm sun melts white frost, birds show delight,
For two thousand years, Time garnered no loss.
Fine flowers on the hanging moss blossom
Only once, when they're being harvested;
Their colouring turns out reinvested,
White dew's repetition reglosses them.
At unfortunate times when lovers meet,
And action on the seaweed expanse fades,
The person being loved, after long delay,
Wishes to know that something will repeat!
St Oswald and angels, St Michael's,
Watch over us, caught in life's loved cycle.

SNOW ON QUINAG

Easter Sunday, Polcraig, 15 April 1990

*V**ides ut alta stet nive candidum*
Quinag: the wind gusts in the chimney,
On dark loch water hail hisses stingingly,
Oystercatcher One pipes his flock to come.
Four electric bars make the bedroom glow,
No peat smokes where we huddle afternoons,
Fire-placed; skidding, the wet track maroons
Our car, on the blown Minch harried clouds grow.
Resplendent wheatears tell us spring is here,
Blue-skied, the sun shines, sallowed dunnocks court,
Countess Seaforth tar-fired the Brahan Seer.
Niru sama, spearing irises grow tall,
Three to four inches, russet heather sports
Green shoots, wagtails pair-bond; I'm here at call.

SNOW ON QUINAG

Thursday 31 October 1991

Bess lies asleep on the cold slab terrace.
Bridges, Masefield, Graves, Blunden, Nichols lived
On Arnold's, Clough's Boars Hill; names poetry gives,
The *Daily Mirror* called it Parnassus.
Artemis steps stiff-nippled from the pool,
Leaves carpet the dark water, wind-stippled;
Deer hide in copses where the background dapples,
Cyclamen in grass promise renewal.
From oaks by the terrace a woodcock rises,
Silently curving over bronze bracken;
Our cocker puppy made no apprises.
From brambles see that put-up pheasant plode,
Through woods and hills Meg's pace never slackens.
Tonight at our door gold pumpkin glows.

SNOW ON QUINAG

Friday 18 September 1992

M ISTY this warm morning, walking stubble fields:
Meg runs ahead, Bess lags the first half;
It feels damp and close taking the copse path,
Swallows twitter, we wait what autumn yields.
Aki no kaze: 'O wha would wish the win
To blaw, or the green leaves fa therewith?' Slow
Dropping of dead leaves where my tractor mows,
Acorns smack the ground, apples turn red-skinned.
Northumberland: low tide at Bamborough,
Mother-of-pearl skies outline Joyous Garde,
Among salty rock-pools busy turnstones stir.
Watashi wa Eikoku no jin desu,
Swinburne's countryman, happily starred;
Clear North Sea water, rippling, murmurs: 'Yes!'

SNOW ON QUINAG

Monday 21 September 1992

Planting hollies in the rain gives pleasure:
Two hundred and fifty-two's the total
So far. It helps through passing years to note all
These things, or they turn forgotten treasure!
Komachi, assist my understanding;
Ueda does say, *Aki no kaze*
Means simply, *aki ni fuku kaze:*
Winter near, do cool airs alter breathing?
Niru sama, look where maple leaves lie
On the damp grass, sometimes in Tatsuta's stream
They redden. I only wish you'd try!
Years do occur when changing months bring sadness;
At times mighty gods share no sweeter dream,
Autumn's gentle breeze brings two hearts gladness.

SNOW ON QUINAG

Friday 25 September 1992

HORACE, our Belgrade cat, sits beside me
On the table, where these books are arranged;
Meg, keen cocker spaniel, out of range
Watching closely: the rain falls endlessly.
That stag's calling lustily for his mate!
Certainly, he doesn't seem cognizant
Of those Man and Woman flowering plants,
That grow on Ono's moor in splendid state!
Favola fui gran tempo, what it is
To be fabulous! I'm quiet at home,
Trying each day to write ten-syllable ditties.
So you've grown up at last, *Niru sama!*
I am pleased, hair shining through the comb,
Myself and your non-Japanese amah!

SNOW ON QUINAG

Tuesday 29 September 1992

OVER the field singing skylarks hover.
Another sunny day; on my Honda
I've mowed for ninety minutes, no wonder,
That way stops you getting hot and bothered.
In Trinity Court a magnolia blows:
Byron kept a bear in his college rooms,
Limping, he swam in the Grantchester pool;
That tall *mokuran* against the west wall grows.
On Sunday Eliza goes to Magdalene:
Benedictine monks from Crowland Abbey
Hostelled here, comfortable, bald men.
Pepys gave Ovid's *Changes*, Caxton-printed.
I wish I had all your *tanka*, gracious lady,
Kokoro ni, in the heart's core imprinted.

SNOW ON QUINAG

Wednesday 21 October 1992

JESSICA, my fair-haired grand-daughter,
Likes gathering leaves, long-stemmed sycamores;
She calls me Pa, all humour she adores,
Awaits a brother or sister quite shortly.
She fell asleep in her belted car-seat,
Did she dream? We walked along the terrace,
I split my finger, a gardening error;
Eclampsia hit when Jess was born, so neat.
The fallow greyhound was outrun on Cotsall:
In one parish, Gitting Barton, Lower Farmcote,
St Faith's roster enshrines the names that fell;
Hailes Abbey's bulk grows cold in the treed distance.
Wit thick as Tewkesbury mustard, that Pointz;
Thin ice on brown puddles shows no persistence.

SNOW ON QUINAG

Wednesday 28 October 1992

Snow whitens Scottish hills, peat stacks covered,
Alert hinds graze quietly: here, sunlight,
Blue skies then rain, *shirotae* leaves glow bright,
The lawn brocade by tractor-strips unravelled.
In the wet field's freezing grass, Meg put up
A cock pheasant; she's bred to do such things.
Overhead, unnoticed, skylarks sing.
In Cotsal folds rams wait the chance to tup:
Will Squele was a Cotswold man, a swinge-buckler;
At Clement's Inn with lusty Justice Shallow,
They knew the bona robas, no sticklers.
Pigs once grunted where our Boars Hill house stands,
Romans built villas, pottery kilns glowed:
Civilizations grow in fertile lands.

SNOW ON QUINAG

Monday 9 November 1992

I LIT the bonfire last night, the bright moon full,
Nozzled hose ready, surroundings raked;
Two years' accumulation flared sparking flakes,
Radiating heat, the east wind barely cool.
The whole family watched, excepting Lize,
Three grandchildren enchanted by the blaze;
Antonia has filled her nine months phase,
Hearts' hopes scintillating in the night sky.
Heat waves shimmer over Adashino:
I want to be remembered, not go
Briefly into the dark, extinguished so.
Countenance William Visor of Wincot
Against the hill's Clement Perks. Moons round slow,
The new baby born will make four, not a lot!

SNOW ON QUINAG

Tuesday 17 November 1992

WHITE sorbus discolor berries cluster
Like snowflakes, tractor tyre-marks freeze over;
The trees stand largely bare, thick pullover
Needed, walking where wet leaves wait clustered.
These are Godless days, no cricket crackles
In the empty hearth; have the Nine Kings gone
To hear that Sutra with the Grand Demon?
On the green-mossed oak sunlight sparkles.
Eliza is nineteen years old today,
Seventeen eleven seventy three's
The day friends gave her midnight bumps, she says.
Show me the way to Dar Lih! *Niru sama*,
While the Third Concubine taught embroidery,
Lotos-leaved, I keep you from Emma!

BIG GRANT THE BARD

Slaggan, by Aultbea, Loch Ewe, Gairloch
Saturday 7 September 1996

BIG GRANT THE BARD and Sir Hector Mackenzie
Could crack a handful of periwinkles;
Loudly hokking red-throat divers link still
On Rudha Mór, ready for springtime frenzy.
The boat's hull rests high up the sandy beach
In winter, though Christmas mimosas may bloom;
Around the steading black cattle find room
Wind-sheltered, while waves on the piled rocks bleach.
The flowering of the yellow iris
Brings health to my bones; wild celery stands tall
Above the tide-mark; where the brown burn falls,
Skullcap pairs petals which the bright sky mirrors.
Slaggan's deserted now; trout rise in the loch,
Hares lope long-legged on the round, barren Ploc.

BIG GRANT THE BARD

Tuesday 10 September 1996

SPRAT-LOONS and borer dive off Gairloch Ard;
Stunted rowans flame, scarlet-berried,
Hedges show *airneach*, sloes, serried,
Shape dark blue ranks. It's going to rain hard.
Cold air streams from the north, wisps of snipe fall
On rocky headlands, ranked wild geese call
Over An Teallach, steady wings in long haul
Find the Gulf Stream before autumn colours pall.
Soon we'll be seeing *corra-chagailt*,
Sulphurous ashes on a frosty night
In the fireplace; make sure you're capped right,
Shoed right, and have porridge in plenty.
You'll have a white gift when the first snow comes!
Clacharain, stone-chatterers, wagtails stay home.

BIG GRANT THE BARD

Thursday 12 September 1996

G*leann an easain*, past the Moated House:
Iain Dall Mackay, the blind Piper and Bard,
Lived at the steading; a groom's hand marred
Brought the Mackays south, skate proved his prowess.
When Lord Reay died, Iain's Lament enshrined
Waterfall Corrie; Lady Janet's marriage
He celebrated, her lissom carriage
The Ninth Laird's prize, while wedding guests dined.
At Dun Bhorreraig they threw him down a cliff,
Where he fell on his feet; led by the swift *allt*,
He heard grey wagtails tsick below the falls;
The live pipes' skirl made his blood race, skin stiffen.
White water-lilies open in the sun;
Gairloch churchyard holds him, ninety-eight years done.

BIG GRANT THE BARD

Saturday 14 September 1996

TWITCHING the curtain disturbs dawn muntjacs:
The radiators grow warm each morning,
The sun descends in the blue sky, pawning
Fertile summer's growth to fetch the next spring back.
To bleach green linen steep it in cow dung!
Her neck's like cotton grass out on the hill,
Twin breasts like foam that low-topped waves spill
On the shell sand, soft hills from a snow blouse sprung.
Camas froineach, that's the bay of ferns,
Lodestar of existence fresh from the sea,
Haven where at evening my long boat turns.
Walbran drowned after grayling in a spring spate
On the Yore, horse nor boat availed his state;
At the Royal Exchange forty-four ate.

BIG GRANT THE BARD

Wednesday 18 September 1996

NEAT, chewed heaps of horse chestnut casings
Dot the grass, withered leaves begin to fall,
The rowans turn golden now; puddings are all
Blackberry and apple, with cream lacing.
Alfred Austin was born at Headingley,
Knew a water cricket when he saw one:
'They went across the veldt,' Jameson Raid done,
'As hard as they could pelt,' said jinglingly.
'While the blue smoke curled in the frosty air,'
He also wrote; he loved his garden
At Swinford Old Manor. The Field Pool at Barden
Lister liked best, a twenty-fish bag his share.
Austin held: 'Nothing can match, where'er we roam,'
True, 'an English wife in an English home.'

BIG GRANT THE BARD

Monday 23 September 1996

Equinox past, we're shielded from hot summer:
Lone swallows hurtle over stubble fields,
Brown trout still wake ratchets on creaking reels;
Autumn's prizes fall to the first comer.
I bought Jess and Hattie candy-floss
At the Newbury Show, saw the MP.
Tears fell because a Shetland turned naughty,
Her slim frame couldn't show who was boss.
Jess shared a pen with a Gloucester Old Spot;
Angela remembered they used to keep
A Saddleback, most pigs stretched asleep;
Suffolk rams showed sturdiest of the lot.
I bought Longmorn; McDowall attested,
Mixed with Smith's and a dash of Clynelish, the best yet!

BIG GRANT THE BARD

Monday 30 September 1996

SHAGGY inkcaps rise between cool terrace slabs:
Meg, wagging her tail, returns, carrying
Proudly a Scots pine-cone; tarrying
Tatsutahime applies colour dabs.
In Velabrum they sold cheese and oil,
Where boats once put in from the wide Tiber:
O San Giorgio benedetto,
Piano voi diceste si; love coils.
Tibullus pictured a girl returning
From her country lover, rich in fine flocks,
Holding a white lamb, from snow-white stock,
Her heart still filled with countryside yearning.
By Saturn's Temple day waited, lingering;
At Santa Sabina's bells rang squilling.

TÜRKIYE

Friday 5 September 1997

CRICKETS call at night like systems bleeping,
Black Sea breezes blow down the Bosphorus;
At noon, with the Hippodrome before us,
White storks glide over, their summer-time keeping.
Crazy Ibrahim's women in the pool
Disported round the cascading fountain;
Hai Sophia's ladies listened doubting
To the preacher exceeding polite rules.
In the Blue Mosque I wore Michael's green socks,
Evliya's father scripted the West Gate:
In the silver sea, England's royal state
Endures, into the island's fabric locked.
A hoopoe paced the path below the wall,
Where Bayram sheep pass live grave-flowers sprawl.

TÜRKIYE

Thursday 11 September 1997

SWERVING swallows make rings, sipping the green pool
Where we swim each day; the marbled terrace
Glows warm out of the wind. Zeus Ourios
Was entreated for aid, where breezes cool.
Massed fishing boats have circled, netting all day,
In the blue-green Bosphorus; we bought bluefish
At the supermarket, an autumn dish,
As plane-tree leaves fall at Sulemaniye.
With a Winged Genius, Jason gave thanks
In Istinye, ending Amycus' pranks
At Beykoz; trim-sailing *Argo*'s lean flanks
Still wait in the harbour over gangplanks.
St Daniel lived on a stone column
For thirty-four years, there he lost volume!

TÜRKIYE

Wednesday 1 October 1997

OVER Boars Hill the jackdaws flock like Dante's,
Chacking in chorus, some wheel remaining:
Meg feeds on dog-laurel fruit, dark-staining,
Fresher weather provokes fast-run antics.
Afiyet olsun! Let there be good health,
Pleasant eating! Half-loaves with mackerel,
Raw onion by Galata Bridge, dark mussels
Proffered in baskets. May there be super-wealth!
Ziyade olsun! At the burial ground,
Where Karaja Ahmet lies in Asia
Sharing the Prophet's earth, mussel shells grace
Women's tombstones, where petalled flowers are found.
Ömrünüz çok olsun! May your years be long!
Living beauty last in this poet's song!

TÜRKIYE

Sunday 19 October 1997

THE inn-sign shrills like a gull in the wind,
Silence otherwise, except for the fire
Ceaseless in the grate. What do hearts desire?
Settled ways, togetherness without stint?
The Hammonds lived here for four hundred years,
Until Nellie Hammond died alone;
All those fresh changes that the old disown,
Ensure transmuting of known things felt dear.
Plovers flute on the fell where settlements show,
Stone Age huts held life enclosed; in the dale
Your fresh loveliness makes living hearts quail,
Warmly responsive under feet of snow.
After long walks we're both bathed and clean;
Lady, the City's stir shows where you have been!

WHEN YOU ARE OLD

Friday 19 December 1997

WHEN you are old and grey and full of sheep
And seated by the fire, page through this book
And slowly read, and dream of the clear look
Your eyes had once, incipient Bo Peep.
How Ronsard saw your movements' passing grace,
And praised your beauty with words false or true,
Unable to cognize a soul in you,
Responsive to your keenly glowing face.
Bent and decrepit you'll traverse the room,
Precariously aged and stumbling,
While your damp lips tremble, faintly mumbling,
Muttering his verses which will mark your tomb.
Live each day freely, forget tomorrow,
This bromeliad's blushing column borrow!

WHEN YOU ARE OLD

Tuesday 23 December 1997

On mild nights moths cluster on the cold panes,
Drawn by the light: owls start hooting early;
The days are quiet, winter's not turned surly,
Through hours of darkness the shining moon wanes.
The tardy cock announces day is here!
In the long winter nights I dream you're here,
Stark naked in my arms you do appear,
There's nothing that you refuse me, my dear!
Some say that ever 'gainst that season comes,
The bird of dawning singeth all night long:
Your ivory body's rose my words' song
Proclaims, how your living loveliness thrums!
Such is midwinter's bed-warmed harvest,
When the larder's full and soft bodies undressed!

WHEN YOU ARE OLD

Monday 22 May 2000

Close up your scarlet petals, Pimpernel,
Rain showers veil the Downs, loosing grey sails
This way over the Vale; the blue sky's veiled,
Long grass overwhelms the fading bluebells.
Cockchafers blunder still about the house
After three years underground; down the lawn
Garden Chafers make their flights, a dark swarm,
Chests iridescent, abdomen a bronze case.
How capable the computer proves to be,
You can read, write, draw, paint, make quick notes,
Record your voice, your correspondence devote
To e-mail, travel the internet for free.
Rain stopped me mowing this afternoon,
Clinging clematis needs more climbing frame room.

WHEN YOU ARE OLD

Imir Fada, Friday 30 August 2002

WHERE the aircraft crashed the six are buried,
Under a white cross, on that long green stretch
Below Ben More; there August sea-pinks arch
Their drooping heads, brief seasons pass unhurried.
April thirteen, sixty-one years ago,
Into the long expanse of time they went
Among the wreck of their passing, intent
On life in fleeting months when fresh hopes grow.
White snow lay on the crests when they died:
This summer noon, stillness holds all the hills;
On the Hill of Springs red deer step at will,
Life and eternity in tandem tied.
Where Neilina and Hectorina were set
At Inchnadamph, their names claim our hearts' debt.

BY SEMER WATER

Monday 29 June 1998

Two greying couples walked by Semer Water
With a camcorder; when they returned
The camera had gone, their heads had turned
White, their legs become trembling transporters.
They did not see us sitting by the ford,
That Romans cobbled through the peat-brown stream.
A curlew whauped, hovering anxiously,
Over green bulrushes where her young deployed.
A reed bunting clung to a swaying stem,
In the breeze that rippled the beck-side meadow:
There bright-pink cuckoo-flowers' spread shows
Ragged until August reaps them low again.
In dark December swans slide along the ice,
Unheard by the dead beneath that carapace.

BY SEMER WATER

Tuesday 25 August 1998

The radiators came on this morning,
Autumn's cool plushness asserts itself now;
We walk gold stubble not yet dark-ploughed,
Meg flushes pheasants along the muck-straw line.
White dew at the field-edge signs Autumn's name,
With coat and cap I fend the cooler air,
Free from summer's heats no salt sweat appears:
This month's changes brings harvest just the same.
The temperature's eighty in Istanbul,
Above Istinye fresher breezes blow:
Through the blue Bosphorus faster currents flow
Past Marmara, striking Gelibolu;
Chonuk Bair and Sakkaria River,
In the fall breeze grasses and water shiver.

BY SEMER WATER

Wednesday 9 September 1998

WE scanned along Scamander as we lunched,
Over the plain towards Achilles' Tomb:
North of the Dardanelles monuments loom,
British, French, Turkish marks of battle-crunch.
Glad girls washed long gowns beside those springs
Below the Scaean Gate, where Hector fell:
Zeus' oak shaded us; hard to spell out
What pain the fall of well-walled cities brings.
Wind-blown fig trees grow on the Eastern Wall,
Bee-eaters flute quippingly as they glide:
They say Hecuba became a lost dog, died
Across the Straits, where later soldiers fell.
That yellow land-caltrop spikes its fruit with thorns;
Stubble stretches where they harvested the corn.

BY SEMER WATER

Wednesday 9 September 1998

SEPTEMBER's early storm brings bevies of quail,
Small and deliciously plump! *Niru sama*,
Though I know the bonds of your English karma,
Moors grow tangled, waiting for love's e-mail!
Our water's metered now: grey-clouded skies
Loose spear-flights of rain, the garden's sopping:
On the Peninsula they fought unstopping,
Where the fallen mostly died their corpses lie.
Skew Bridge and the Redoubt: the RND
Withered away in khaki like dead leaves,
Collingwood fell to the ground; where flies heave
The bodies swell, until spades earth them free.
The spear struck Aphareus on the throat,
His head hung to one side, no homeward-bound boat.

BY SEMER WATER

Wednesday 14 October 1998

WATER flowed down Park Scar on the stony track
After yesterday's downpour: leafed ashes swayed
Against a blue sky that the west wind flayed;
Angela cut her knee, her shin's blue-black.
When I chose beauty, you proved my reward:
Aphrodite's guerdon, shapeliness preferred,
Hera and Pallas felt their anger stir;
Paris took Leda's girl, Helen, on board.
Lady, you tumbled down my city-walls,
When the salt-stained ships stranded on the sand;
Even grey elders, feeling the spell you dispense,
Thought you worth keeping, your decrepit thralls!
You rebuild my love's tower mortar-free,
Then give me Yorkshire fruit-cake for my tea!

BY SEMER WATER

Thursday 24 June 1999

EVERYTHING needed a good watering
When we got back home, the peonies most.
Monks who made green pastures their living hosts,
They called *boskoi*, hands unstained by slaughtering.
Up on the moor stiff soft rush stems clatter
In the north-west wind, the heather shows dark,
No sun shines through there; long rush-lights sparked
Cobbett's youth, no sound of *lagopus* matters.
From a black cow's vulva thin legs extend,
She stands there grazing, shifting restlessly!
Walking the Dales each day, progressively
Adds calf-muscle mass, this long-walked fells lend!
Niru sama, moors grow more tangled left to lie,
Conversely tissue swells each time it plies!

BY SEMER WATER

Friday 25 June 1999

Come down, covenanter, from green-plovered hills,
My heart's dragoons scour for you, riding hard;
No black-backed gull can your labours mar,
No lime-flushed wild flowers hold you enthralled.
Your covenant's here, where douce grey houses stand,
Decorous flowers brightening each stone wall:
That round-arched window lets sunlight fall
Into landing and hall, one woman manned!
Melancholy thistle was your emblem,
At first drooping low, then standing up tall;
Now silence and country peace full days recall,
All past sorrows these rustic pleasures stem:
Brown trout from the river, meadow lamb again,
New-cut Wensleydale, fresh-sprung champagne!

BY SEMER WATER

Saturday 23 October 1999

For your first birthday they gave you a bear
On wheels, to push or ride; strong hands held you on:
At sixty-five, I watch the rain come on
Across the vale; bright sun has smaller shares!
'Love from Jimmy,' you wrote on a photo
Of you in three-piece suit and Eton collar,
And Lowland bonnet. When our shared mother
Remarried, you knew where your love flowed to.
Two brothers added, when she sailed back
On Home Leave, what did hungry hearts feel?
Snow-salted, you held the bannets, sturdy chiel,
Headed a bicker, fast hurdler up the track.
Kittle Nine Steps face us down the ages,
Castle Rock fox-holes or Parnassus pages.

BY SEMER WATER

Saturday 23 October 1999

STIRLING CASTLE guards the Highland highways,
Argyll and Sutherland Highlanders' depot:
High School Head Boy, a different bonnet shows
Towered, badged, token of dangerous days!
Lorne Campbell's Seventh Battalion moved north
To Nairn for training, above the Moray Firth:
A fine moustache asserts your first pip's worth,
Photographed at Elgin, at officers' course,
Signed 'To Mummy with best love, from Jimmy.'
At Elgin Cottage, Aunt Kate dictated
Bread and butter before permitted cake!
Henryson walked by Dunfermline Abbey,
'Christ heis law hairtis and lawis he':
The winds blow all away save constancy.

BY SEMER WATER

Saturday 23 October 1999

'Ane doolie sessoun to ane cairfull dyte
Suld correspond, this in myne oratur:
From the cold North haill gan discend in showers;
Richt sa it wes quhen I began to wryte.'
'Under this stane lait Lipper lyis deid.'
Lorne Campbell won his DSO in lost France;
His compass-work by night, against all chance,
Brought two companies through uncaptured.
Eleventh in a soldier's family line,
His grandfather's grandfather founded the Argylls;
His Seventh Battalion faced future trials,
Where Rommel's armour tracked in massed design.
'The nicest man in Scotland,' he was called,
His said 'Well done!' the finest words of all.

BY SEMER WATER

Saturday 23 October 1999

THE battalion route-marched through Cape Town,
Pipes skirling, stretching long-convoyed legs;
Our mother sent us on short-trousered legs
To meet him at Kenilworth station, half-grown!
Way down the platform a tall figure stood,
Green tartan kilted, badger-sporraned:
'Are you Second Lieutenant Gilmour?', stunned,
We asked. He laughed, he was all he should.
How our mother managed I cannot tell:
He sat on the floor, revealing just a kilt;
We stood proudly beside him, shadows spilt
Into his photograph, all would be well!
Shielded by Scots regiments, how could we lose?
Eager to stand in those well-polished shoes.

BY SEMER WATER

Saturday 23 October 1999

HE found the Cape Town ladies well forward,
When officers were dined at Kelvingrove!
Married himself, he saved his heart for love,
Keeping what he had to proffer in store.
Every morning gold light fell on the dunes,
Birds scattered through a clarity of air:
Every officer has a duty of care
For his men, piped to military tunes.
Centre lines were lit through successive mine-belts,
Amber indicated danger, green meant safe;
Plumes of dust trailed where loud Valentines raced,
Learning to give the enemy a welt!
Grants and Shermans provided muscle,
Planes overhead evidenced hustle.

BY SEMER WATER

Monday 25 October 1999

AT VIMEIRO they advanced in three lines,
Bagpipes playing, Junot's men retired:
At El Alamein they went up through the wire,
Ear-marked for assault, their morale high.
Dunbar: 'Timor mortis conturbat me:'
Prudence, 'Quhy wald thow hald that will away,
On that journay going everie day?'
Eight eighty-two guns blasted their barrage that day.
A ground-set bomb wiped out a whole platoon:
They took Greenock, making the Black Line sure;
A and B came up with Valentines, skewered
By mines, far from yellow irises of June.
'Hast thou beheld a peal of ordnance strike?'
Enemy guns sent schours of mortall haill in spikes.

BY SEMER WATER

Monday 25 October 1999

THEY went up against One Sixty-Four Light:
At eleven p.m., in bright moonlight,
They attacked southwest from Greenock, straight
For strong Nairn, no barrage, bayonets shone bright.
In their weapon-pits sixty Germans died,
A Company lost all its officers.
'Patience sayis: Let Fortoun wirk furthe her rage,
Quhill that hir glas be run; nane uther way besyde,
Sayis Deid, my yettis wyd sall the abyd.'
'Than sayis Age to me, My freind, cum neir:
Cum, brodir, tak my hand, thow hes compt to mak
Off all thi tyme thow spendit heir.'
Lorne Campbell wrote: 'His loss we share,
His men would have followed him anywhere.'

BY SEMER WATER

Monday 25 October 1999

We spent the summer at Mara, shadowed
By death, in an apple-treed Elgin farmhouse.
'Why is she blubbing?', I asked, at a loss,
Perplexed by tidings that I did not know.
The tall farmer rode up to visit us,
Leather-booted, carrying a twelve-bore:
He'd shot a hawk, gave us, a young boy's chore,
The corpse to bury; we were nonplussed;
After a while we dug it up again,
Stunned by a seething mass of maggots.
I cut my finger to the bone, bled lots;
The budgie escaped, was never seen again.
The dam we swam in was a peaty-brown;
Diving, Ian bled, scraped from toe to crown.

BY SEMER WATER

Monday 25 October 1999

From our bedroom window at Kinlochard,
We saw Ben Lomond standing white with snow:
From the Castle Rock shining bugles blow;
Your name's in the book, bones where desert winds pass.
'In Dunfermelyne Deid hes done roune
With Maister Robert Henrysoun:' death stalks.
What consolation does our frailty baulk,
Clinging at dusk to an evening star?
Days of heavy rain have brought the leaves down,
Revealing buds ready for next year's spring;
The sun shines this morning, hearts wakening,
Courage enlivens even fortune's frown.
'Brother, you'll step through just as I have done,
War's bridges crossed, life's fulfilment won.'

BY SEMER WATER

Wednesday 27 October 1999

Meg found nothing, quartering the set-aside:
After the Nairn action, Doctor Wilson
And his stretcher-bearers, questing keenly
Like spaniels, got all the wounded away.
At Westonbirt Arboretum colours flare:
The maple leaves on Stand Up Field hillside
Make a deep-crimson Chinese brocade design;
Gold and scarlet mingle everywhere.
'As a priest of the redeeming Buddha,
I keep my frail heart strictly controlled;
But seeing a marsh-snipe start up, I know
The full effect of autumn's evening shadows'.
Io fugendo vo de sasso in sasso,
E la morte risponde al basso al basso.

BY SEMER WATER

Thursday 2 December 1999

THE Leyburn road runs up Whipperdale Bank,
Through DANGER AREAS, past tracks made for tanks:
By Black Beck Bridge, grouse butts off to one flank,
Red grouse appeared, survivors giving thanks.
Through Redway Head we drove down to Grinton:
In St Andrew's churchyard Cadet Barton lies,
RAF, November nineteen eighteen;
Up the dale merlins speed down the wind's run.
Bleak House stands perched high above Swaledale,
Where the road climbs steeply to Windgate Greets;
The sun painted gold by the Roman street
On to Semer Water, where welcome failed.
It proved more than a Yorkshire Wee-bit,
Passing greener fells haunted by peewits.

THE JACKDAW FLOCK

Wednesday 29 December 1999

THE jackdaw flock under their leader's care
Wings back to Boars Hill over frost-white fields;
Some circle away for the warm byre's yield:
'My prime of youth was but a frost of cares.'
We are risen now to the seventh splendour,
The happy sphere where golden Saturn reigns;
My Lady leads me there, loosing my pain,
Laying bare what tranquillity engenders.
If She were to smile on me with full intent,
I'd be turned to ash like Semele.
Here in the heaven to which *noi sem levati*,
I'd be a branch that lightning's brilliance rent.
In Saturn's happy world all turns out best,
Where blest security brings warm hearts rest.

THE JACKDAW FLOCK

The Century's End, Friday 31 December 1999

How still it is, the last day of the year
And century in which so many died:
Mist veils all the wet fields, cock pheasants strive
To tame their rivals for the coming year.
Curlew, piping lonely in the cold dale,
Be still for a while: let the young man lay
His head on her knees, life withers away
Like dry sedge tapping in the wind's trail;
Her dead brother's courage example still,
Strong heart unfailing and unbroken will.
Down Kettlewell Beck peaty fell waters spill
Into the heavy Wharfe running at will.
Bring the Christmas tree, champagne's wine-breath:
Along scoured banks dippers plan New Year nests.

THE JACKDAW FLOCK

Tuesday 4 January 2000

Glimpsed through dripping fog all seems changed:
Is this the most unblest Cimmeria?
Youths, and their wives, much suff'ring aged men,
Boot-plopped grasses, become something strange.
'God tempers the cold wind to the shorn lamb:'
That's a French proverb, used by Laurence Sterne.
Is it from sage ancestors that we learn?
Do friendly spirits hold us in light hands?
Ambarvalia! This is no good time
To slop about wet fields! Seek fit lustration,
When suns fill blue skies with coruscations,
No faint ghosts answer though you call three times.
Even Achilles hid from war's harsh call,
Enlisting Deidameia among love's thralls.

THE JACKDAW FLOCK

Monday 10 January 2000

SHALL I compare you to a winter's day?
You are too warming and more intricate;
Cold airs do freeze the Janus buds today,
And winter's long nights display too dark a state.
Sometimes too faint the eye of heaven shines,
And often is his golden glory dimmed;
And other fairs from best fairs do decline,
By fate from beauty's fine perfection trimmed.
But your cool body's fitness shall not fade,
Nor lose possession of the face you show us;
Death shall not brag you work out in his shade,
For in my lasting lines your grace moves best!
So long as men can sigh or eyes can see,
So long you'll live, verse's own currency.

THE JACKDAW FLOCK

Friday 14 January 2000

The frost coats fallen branches, not the ground:
From brittle rape-stems Meg puts skylarks up;
Briskly cheerful, they flirt wings through the murk,
Chirping overtures to spring's swelling sounds.
My mistress's eyes are nothing like the sun,
Lips not coral red; snow's white, her breasts are dun!
Are hairs wires? Gold wires bedeck her bright head,
On her snowy cheeks rose petals have bled.
I think I never saw a goddess go:
But my lithe mistress puts on a perfect show,
Walk and aspect adapted where she goes;
What gifts she bears my own reaction knows!
Two goldfinches forage the lemon balm,
Pair-bonding in them subsumes entire charms.

THE JACKDAW FLOCK

Polesden Lacey, Thursday 20 January 2000

'L̲OVE gilds the scene, and women guide the plot.'
Dick Sheridan fought two duels for her,
Recovering from the second took a year;
Style and undaunted courage, 'damn'd or not'!
Thomas Cubitt's south colonnade still stands
At Polesden Lacey, he developed
Belgravia. Now the North Downs envelop
William McEwan's wealth, stylish not grand.
The yellow stuccoed walls show up warmly
Against green grass in grey January;
Paintings, panelling grace this Greville granary,
Beauty's managed face shows here charmingly.
Stubborn gallantry, unaltered manners,
Iron self-control outface the world's clamour.

THE JACKDAW FLOCK

St David's Day, Wednesday 1 March 2000

THE blue Downs curve against an eggshell sky,
Changing clouds vary their fleecy patterns;
Across the Vale dark rafts float rain-battered,
Cock pheasants duel over territory.
Space Jason and his Cybernauts we sail
Through illimitable air, unhorizoned
To Hospitable seas, bedizened
With megaherz and gigabytes! Hours fail.
Snowdrops have lighted the way, hail chilled;
Now Angela picks toppling daffodils,
Angled by sun and wind, their long stems spill
Gold bullion for March to treasure at will.
Victorian historians, armed
With Morality, carry Clio's palms!

KARAYEL WAS BLOWING

Tuesday 21 March 2000

KARAYEL was blowing when we landed,
Layering black cloud over the City:
Antonia and the girls met us sweetly,
Rebooting what the meeting's hour demanded.
A hooded crow bathed next dawning
In the boat-shaped, sea-blue paddling pool.
Above the shrubby cemetery life rules,
Flocking tree sparrows bustle here each morning.
The wolf will snatch the isolated lamb,
Shepherd not by! Before Kurban Bayram,
Sheep and cattle wait penned; Abraham
Spared his son Isaac and sacrificed a lamb.
That beauty's eye-lashes move, sharp-pointed,
With life-raising power she is anointed!

KARAYEL WAS BLOWING

Tuesday 28 March 2000

VANESSA PREIIA, we adore in you
Nature's bounty, and the seasons' beauty:
Grain, wine, game, fruit, flowers sweeten duty,
Sea-fish, and trout from Cestros' Aksu.
Artemis Pergaia, we revere in you
Our city's stature! Your lovely temple
We raised to praise you; your Demiurge still
Builds for you, more than plain citizens do.
Cestros, the river god, leans on his rock,
His crown's real grass, river amphora-sourced:
Plancia Magna, your Fortune's free course
Flowed, your statue shows your beauty's stock.
We drank spring water under the bare vine,
While the Anatolian sheepdog watched, supine.

KARAYEL WAS BLOWING

Wednesday 29 March 2000

Nesil drove us to the Eurymedon,
The Kopru Chay and the Nehir restaurant;
We sat in the sun by the blue-green current,
While a circling buzzard eyed goings-on.
Afiyet olsun! River trout for lunch,
Tomato and cucumber. To the north,
Snow-covered mountains showed us the sun's worth,
White background to the new, warm season's crunch.
On the acropolis, we heard loud knocks
Beside the anemones and asphodel;
Love-hungry tortoises bashing their shells,
The hot sun unfastening winter's locks.
We rubbed on sun-cream, fresh from sunless days,
Hearts expanding to give appropriate praise!

KARAYEL WAS BLOWING

Thursday 30 March 2000

TINKLING sheep bells ring among the ruins
On the acropolis, above asphodel
And anemone carpets. All went well
Once, the fame of their horses accruing;
Lemon-wood furniture scented their trade.
The epitaph by the river's mouth says:
'Killed by the Median bowmen, praise
These spearmen; their manhood's lost splendour weigh!'
'Hadley's Harem' came down in the summer sea
During the war, bombardier dead, engines gone;
Captain and co-pilot drowned, their cockpit's shown
In the Koç Museum, Starfighter perched featly.
At the Gloria Golf Resort Hotel
We ended the day, bed made for backs that play!

KARAYEL WAS BLOWING

Monday 3 April 2000

Fit time has come to celebrate the spring,
Season to which lovers and poets respond,
And all warm nature! From winter's despond
We wake, in answer to the sun's caressing.
Antonia and Paul went off to play golf
At seven-thirty, leaving the girls with us;
An hour's breakfast gave a happy surplus,
Then ball games by the gently frothing surf.
A crested lark foraged between bare poles,
A white sea-plane floated on the green cut,
A Maule M6, ready to taxi-up
Into the wind, feeling the air's control.
We went indoors to the rotunda pool,
Seeing through glass the sun exert his rule.

KARAYEL WAS BLOWING

Monday 3 April 2000

By the blue-watered pool the mobile rang,
The golfers were returning, one jubilant,
One not! They'd seen the spring's migrants,
Swallows and swifts as the white golf balls sprang!
After lunch in the sun, blue loungers beckoned
By the outdoor pool; common bulbuls fluted
In shrubs and palms; Herodotus mooted
Several opinions, choosing the sound.
After French cricket on the beach, I spotted
A brown bump in the waves, drifting closer,
One turtle head then two, in love's closeness,
Eagle-beak mouthed, distinctively brown-spotted.
She seemed underwater rather a lot,
Old Man of the Sea, love's piggy-back he got!

KARAYEL WAS BLOWING

Monday 10 April 2000

WHEN gold celandines sow brocade carpets,
The swallows arrive, mountains white with snow;
By Manavgat falls sheepdog puppies grow,
Suckling still they have no sorrows to forget!
Gladiators died in Sidé's theatre,
To please the crowd. We walked the high street
To the Liman restaurant, platters fish-replete,
Near the moon goddess's temple, love-waker.
Anthony and Cleopatra met here
By the salt, warm sea, married in Antakya,
Lost love's empire, political distraction!
Over blue waves her gold galley appeared.
The Airbus flew crammed full for Istanbul,
Where snow lined the roadsides, distinctly cool!

KARAYEL WAS BLOWING

Wednesday 12 April 2000

WHEN you're not thinking of me, my heart changes
To a desert, where djinns throw javelins:
Movement's a blessing but, Lady, restrain
Your froings, that the City's ways derange!
When Boreas is raising no hubbub,
Steer your brightly painted *taka* to the shore,
Deeply cargoed with earth's fertile store,
Wine, vegetables and fruit, white yoghurt in tubs!
Drink five cups of wine, as digestion requires!
Snow fell heavily while we ate fish and chips,
Yorkshire-style, in Etiler; how short hours slip,
Family-shared, further visits desired!
Paul drove gingerly down the icy hill,
BA's 767 rose with a will.

THE FALLING RAIN

Thursday 3 August 2000

THE falling rain makes me think of the Lifra,
Whose creeks the incoming tide turned into pools:
On the horizon space and emptiness rule,
Outward-bound freighters write their smoke's cipher.
The Liver Bird rules building and city,
St John the Evangelist's golden eagle:
Now Liverpool Victoria inveigles
Our house insurance, sound statistically!
Arthur Hugh Clough was born in Rodney Street,
A cotton merchant's son, Arnold's Thyrsis
And Rugby's: to meet Time's reaper, Lityerses,
Matthew went; Dingle Lane stilled his heartbeats.
'Ho THEOS meta sou!' Highland lassie
Or Oxford, coarse poortith Clough didn't fancy!

THE FALLING RAIN

Thursday 14 September 2000

Winds bring down the lip-red berry clusters,
That fend winter's darkness from the warm house:
Witches and bogles hate their bright carouse,
In those green rauns all summer's strength musters.
When winds hold loud sway during dowly months,
Gusting and howling for dree weeks on end,
When the windows rattle and peat smoke bends,
It's hard to recall kinder circumstance.
Snow on the hills and the loch never still,
Great northern divers on deep Eriboll,
Below the Wheelhouse and the Souterrain,
The smoored peat fire winks fragrantly still.
From the box-bed we hear the wind's raging,
Restless background to your beauty's staging.

THE FALLING RAIN

Thursday 19 September 2000

Rob Donn praised Glen Golly's green birches:
When his strength began to fail, he buried
His favourite gun on Ben Spionnaidh; he's laid
To rest in Balnakeil, where the church ruin is.
Past Lochan Fionnlaidh, above dark Doire Dhu
We climbed to the col steeply through heather:
Sweet-tasting blueberries lightened the weather,
On the wide col the gale's gusting strengths grew.
We struggled up into the wind's kingdom,
For they shall mount up with wings as eagles;
Inverpolly's stark peaks inveigled
Our far-seeing eyes into air strong wings thrum.
We reached the summit on hands and knees,
Every two steps the gale turned into three.

THE FALLING RAIN

Monday 30 October 2000

WHEN every boot-fall re-echoes splashing,
And green ash leaves supply soft cushioning,
And winds blow dark rain clouds in succession,
Then ways are clarty and the weather clashy.
Floudby days when the storms are feeding,
And flaycrahs lose their last scraps of clothing,
Then the catawse glow red for backend's cheering,
While the wind-stripped trees last leaves are shedding.
Are you dowly today? Red choops are glowing;
Sit yourself somewhere dry and bieldy,
Where fire glows warm and the wind's force fielded,
Away from cah-claps and wet swiddens showing.
I'm maffly just now, there's hope for leetening,
When thoughts of you bring their own sweetening.

THE FALLING RAIN

Monday 6 November 2000

MACPHERSON wrote, 'The public may depend
On the following fragments as genuine
Remains of ancient Scottish poetry!' Spin
Through rain and snow to the appointed end.
Cool Ossian, 'the last of the heroes:'
Courage's fame spreads throughout this new world,
Bay-leaf sprays on the bonfire sound and curl,
Essential oils flare fragrance briefly known.
Chain-sawn oak branches fed the jumping flames,
All the family joined in round the fire:
Golden sparks gilt the dark, marks of desire,
Glowing verse preserved for lasting fame.
People resemble Morven's flying leaves,
When a thousand ghosts by night break the trees.

THE FALLING RAIN

Wednesday 20 December 2000

Five days till Christmas! I've cut some holly,
Brought in fragrant fronds of coned Scots pine:
The tree's all lit up, this evening we'll dine
On smoked eel and organic salmon jelly,
Reminders of windswept Achiltibuie
And the Summer Isles! Small white winter moths
Cling to the windows, cold champagne will froth
Toasting forty-two years of marriage, free
At sixty-seven to think gratefully
Of benefactions, enjoying newly
Read verse, renewed perceptions enduing
Rich days with reaches of long centuries.
Three Kings came to the hay-scented stable,
That Birth more than an angelic fable.

THE FALLING RAIN

Saturday 30 December 2000

Here at the year's cusp in my dressing-gown,
I didder out into the snow's powdering
Like dithering-grass! May longer days bring
Food for the birds, and lighten all that's grown.
The thermostat calls for the busy pump
Continuously, hear the boiler thump
As the Celsius drops; wild creatures lump
The cold, the past year's drab colours they've dumped.
The tiny goldcrests forage in close pairs,
Exiled from their vanished canopy,
Tree-creepers zag in freshened panoply,
White clouds soften the cerulean air.
Two burnished foxes frolic through the wood,
The year's change tells them couple-time comes good.

THE FALLING RAIN

Monday 7 May 2001

When spindly coltsfoot swells to butterbur,
　　Spring's sap runs upward to the chilly air:
Flora declares dominion everywhere,
Pacing fresh green to scatter her bright stars.
Large snowflakes fall like wool on the high fells,
(Horace's line altered), but the bright sun
Melts them into vapour, changed one by one
To blue sky-haunters, where their souls dispel.
On peaty rivers sandpipers file their claims,
'Kitty-weewit' they cry low over the Wharfe;
Their shrilly piping tells rivals 'Please keep off!'
Sandbars and sandy banks assign their name.
I'm your *ver sacrum*, I must go out-by!
On Conistone bridge a squashed sand martin lies.

THE FALLING RAIN

Tuesday 5 June 2001

RAINY FREY has roused fertility
In the frozen earth with long summer days;
Elves proliferate where foxgloves display,
Gambolling fox cubs show agility.
After the solstice meadwort will flavour
Sweet mead cups, marzipan, the frothing flowers
Honey for lovers: for married hours
Sharp-pickle cucumber leaves add their dower.
Lovely Freyja, shapeliest of Vanirs,
Goddess of lovers' nights, you do transmute
Passion into marriage, hearth-fixed roots,
And Friday nights closely married couples find dear.
Thor, take your hammer to Midgard's Great Snake,
May your thunder far from our fresh crops break.

THE FALLING RAIN

Thursday 7 June 2001

The changing months have warmed Gerda's breasts,
Her white arms' glimmer fills the radiant sky,
Her body lights up the murmuring sea:
Only her yielding gave well-horsed Frey rest.
No swallows or martins twitter overhead,
But the hidden nightingale signs her name
To summer's voucher, and true beauty claims
For secret June and happy lovers' beds.
When Gerda baulked, Skirnir gave warning
She'd rattle like a dry thistle on the ice:
Nine nights' delay more than sufficed
For flaming Frey, till her beauty gave sorning.
Fighting giants to win her he lost his sword,
No help in the last ages of the world.

THE FALLING RAIN

Tuesday 26 June 2001

The grass looks green and pleasant, the mowing's done,
Chattering swifts arrowhead through the sky;
Hot, dry weather; I shield my eyes
On the cool terrace just out of the hot sun.
The keen cats have killed a youthful blackbird
And a young blackcap, whose parent was singing
So melodiously; a crow fledgeling
Lies expressionlessly dead on the stony drive.
Only four days till Saturday's wedding,
Rings, wedding dress, flower arrangements made,
Smart suits, a hundred people on display;
Blossoming pots to move for drive-side bedding.
I must learn the speech Angela wrote by heart,
Phrase timing, articulation's the art.

AUTUMN BUSH CLOVER

Saturday 13 February 1993

This open field of autumn bush clover
Is totally lost at red dawn's parting;
I must ask the traveller departing,
When he'll come again with fresh endeavours:
Poet, subject unknown; Honda writes of wasps
Humming. The third Spring song's much the same:
Where's that spring mist gone? With its lovely name,
Mi-Yoshino's Happy Moor has snow, lots!
There's a spring mist here all right! Nitrogen
Sulphur dioxides taint the atmosphere.
Some characters come straight from *kyôgen:*
Koman and co. hold hemp-threading baskets;
Hemp and dawn are affined, it seems,
Hemp stalks wilt under excessive tasking.

AUTUMN BUSH CLOVER

Monday 1 March 1993

I KNOW nothing to hold on to, this dawn:
Is it worth trying whether life still
Exists for us? Shall I forget past thrills?
Repeated visits seem to make him yawn.
Although swelling spring's presence is quite clear,
There's no plum scent in my hill hamlet:
The bush warbler's singing in a scambled
Voice, waiting for better times to appear!
Immortal goddess, in your snowy woods
Hurdling bronze bracken to the stricken deer,
Actaeon loved your beauty as he stood.
Our pink plum blossoms have turned snow-white;
The snowy path showed Meg a moorhen near,
Adorned with dead bracken, she was a sight.

AUTUMN BUSH CLOVER

Tuesday 16 March 1993

NEITHER poet nor subject assigned:
A thousand peachy thigh-birds are calling,
That it's swelling springtime: the appalling
Thing is; they're all renewed, I'm in decline!
Ki composed this after crossing Meet Slope:
A secondary consideration
After crossing Meet Hill, in valediction,
Is why when men, and any other eyes,
Part at Meeting Hill on saying goodbye,
The name should have acquired its special scope?
Pirngshyh; could I have rested my long arms
On the carriage bar, to write poetry?
Niru sama, when I let my face show slightly,
A certain poet wondered at my charms!

AUTUMN BUSH CLOVER

Friday 19 March 1993

THINKING of a parted friend, who had gone
To Crossing County, Mitsune wrote this:
Homing geese voyage on swelling spring's lift,
Travelling the route where soft white clouds drift;
May they act as a medium between us
With the word-thing, now I'm left on my own.
This, Henjô, an Emperor's great-grandson wrote:
It's difficult enough seeing the way
Through hedges on the hillside where dusk stays:
In full darkness you wouldn't be capable
Of crossing; so I think you'd better stay,
Rather than stumbling, lost, out on the slopes!
In a tall oak tree, against a blue sky,
A warbler called, chiffchaff! chiffchaff! today.

AUTUMN BUSH CLOVER

Monday 22 March 1993

It must happen because I've been picking
A branch of plum blossom that my wide sleeve
Gives off a plum scent; that's why I do believe
There's a bush warbler right here, now, singing.
In the mountain breeze the cherry petals
Blow about in scented confusion:
The flowers' emotional occlusion
May stop us leaving and let us settle.
By the golden gorse the hawthorn's greening;
Spring rain all last night, brief fog this morning;
One crow lines her nest, the other's preening.
Wild cherry's out at the edge of the wood,
Fresh leaves shine beneath heaven's blue awning:
Spring equinox, everything's looking good.

AUTUMN BUSH CLOVER

Tuesday 23 March 1993

I*T'S* not so much the colour, but plum scent
That sends me climbing emotional heights!
Whose plum-incensed sleeve, love's megabyte,
Touched my house's plum tree with such content?
If cherry blossom scent is not enough
To keep you here, perhaps the strongest draw
To bring you back, is the serried store
Of buoyant bloom swaying in the wind's luff!
Lord Chatham could not sufficiently deplore
The use of Indian braves to slaughter
Colonists in the American war.
Only John Wells escaped, at boarding school
In New York; earlier Uncas's daughter
Married Leffingwell: here peace is the rule.

AUTUMN BUSH CLOVER

Wednesday 24 March 1993

It's not a good idea planting a plum tree
With scented flowers by one's residence:
It's a wretched thing to mistake the scent
For the lover expected eagerly!
The tears shed innumerably on parting
Add to the volume of the waterfall:
People below will see a natural
Level of flow, increased by tears starting!
So many Booths have been sepultured
Round Warrington parish church, Lancashire
Born and bred, by corn markets nurtured.
Under a blue sky a nation's treasure grows,
Hallowed fields produce what we require:
Rice seedlings green again round Heiankyô.

AUTUMN BUSH CLOVER

Thursday 25 March 1993

MERELY because I stood for a short while
By the plum blossom, my wife's complaining:
She's gone cold, despite my apt explaining
How that perfume imbued me in fine style!
Ki composed this in Rice Wine Warmer Hall,
After lunch one day, when the sacred wine
Had gone the rounds, deprecating the rain
That was falling while they were enjoying
A stirrup cup. It is most annoying
Seeing bush clover flowers rain drenched;
But my feelings suffer a greater wrench
Leaving Your Highness in the rainy fall.
It's eleven o' clock, my spaniel waits
For milk and a biscuit; she concentrates.

AUTUMN BUSH CLOVER

Tuesday 30 March 1993

To whom if not to you, would I despatch
This spray of plum blossom to please the eye?
As for perfume and coloration, why,
Of *cognoscenti* no one is your mate.
For all your kindnesses unceasingly
Performed, my wet sleeve's white tear-globules
I'll keep wrapped in my sleeve, as nodules
Of remembrance, now that you're leaving me.
Where I sit I see Taihaku flowers,
Largest cherry blossom; which goes to show,
Wait long enough, everything has its hour!
Two muntjacs pace our lawn at early dawn:
At Kingfisher Pool, Angela, you know,
Saw three roe-deer racing round the corner.

AUTUMN BUSH CLOVER

Thursday 1 April 1993

Even in moonlight, you can't really see
Where the plum-tree flowers are blossoming;
It's the peerless scent that keeps you homing in
Mitsune's direction, bright moon on high!
If only the drops gathering together
On the extended bud, would precipitate
As swelling spring rain! While you contemplate
Wearing wet clothes, I'm sure you'd rather stay!
In the misty rain a chaffinch called
Repeatedly in a tall oak's wet branch;
Warblers now move, vocally installed.
Silver stars covered Motomori's hat:
In these damp days crow plumage, rain drenched,
Glistens wetly; can courtiers cap that?

THE THREE-DAY-OLD MOON

Friday 20 April 2001

A WHITE canopy of blossom swells gently
In the chilly air; busy great tits, paired,
Keep on the go, bright sunshine brings them cares
And lightens them: the moon wanes presently.
Over heaven's wide sea cloud-waves rise up:
The three-day-old moon forms a slender boat,
Into a forest of bright stars it floats,
Concealed, rowed through the stars' eye-stop.
I seem to wander erratically
Through a night whose darkness never changes:
My sleeves maintain their inky-black strangeness,
Finding no light of day in which to dry.
The six poets are Homer, Virgil, Horace,
Ovid, Lucan, Dante raised to high place.

THE THREE-DAY-OLD MOON

Monday 23 April 2001

Pear blossom opens in the glistening rain,
The first birds' eggs lie broken on the grass:
Taihaku flowers show largest till they pass,
While Shirotae's snowy clouds remain.
Until this moment I had barely thought
About it, but the comprehension
That this lovely moon will move, hidden,
Sharpens delight, since these hours prove short.
Darling daughter, why should you disappear
So completely into the trackless sky?
Evanescent snowfalls at least supply
Light flakes that settle in the world right here.
St George's Day! The moon has gone to rest,
Appearing soon to make glad mortals blest!

THE THREE-DAY-OLD MOON

Tuesday 8 May 2001

WHITE anemones carpet the Strid Wood,
   Where warblers tell us spring has brought delight:
The trefoil alleluia sees us right
For salads and for heaven, green signs of good.
Even on Borrow-Deepdale's wide expanse,
Where stout-hearted fellows lift their lofty bows
And brandish them about, the moonlight glows,
Spreading a clear light to dispel romance.
Here at the service to remember you,
Daughter, in a frenzy of love's longing,
How ghastly to hear that bell echoing:
Each sounding moment resonates with you.
Romilly and his leashed greyhound slipped,
The successive Wharfe wrestled them at grips.